ALPHA-GAL ALLERGY SYNDROME

A tick disease

Information
Recipes

© Copyright 2021 by R L Boyd

Lynn Alan Publishing. All rights reserved.

I've been living with Alpha-gal for about twenty years. I spent the first twelve years trying to find out why I had these strange symptoms. Finally, after begging to be tested, the diagnosis came back as Alpha-gal. The allergist said to avoid red meats and possibly dairy. That sounded easy but wasn't that simple. I tried to find more information online with very little success. I was thankful to have a diagnosis but frustrated by the lack of knowledge of medical personnel. My hope is that I can help others by sharing what I have learned over the years. I have changed recipes to make them Alpha-gal safe and will share some of those in this book. Thank you to my family and friends for the love and support throughout this crazy journey.

I also thank my Alpha-gal friends on social media groups. They have helped so many simply by sharing their stories about tick diseases including Alpha-gal. I have been encouraged and amazed by their positivity.

Thank you for the opportunity to share information and recipes with anyone willing to learn, including family and friends of Alpha-gal positive people.

What is Alpha-gal Allergy Syndrome?

Alpha-gal Syndrome (AGS) is also called Alpha-gal allergy, red meat allergy, or tick bite meat allergy. It is a serious, potentially life-threatening allergic reaction.

Alpha-gal is a sugar molecule found in most mammals. It is not normally found in fish, reptiles, birds, or people.

That is about all the internet tells us. Alpha-gal only shows up through a blood test. The skin prick test will not tell you if you have AGS.

Beware: Alpha-gal is also in products made from mammals such as cosmetics, soaps, lotions, dairy, gelatin and medication.

Reactions can include rash, hives, nausea, vomiting, difficulty breathing, drop in blood pressure, dizziness or faintness, severe stomach pain, or gastrointestinal symptoms. These reactions can be minimal or severe. The average reaction is reported to be between three to six hours after exposure. The delayed reaction makes it more difficult to diagnose. **Fume reactions -**aka airborne allergens- have been reported in about a third of people with Alpha-gal. While fume reactions may take a little time, it is usually within minutes of exposure.

"Have an EpiPen with you at all times."

Consistently inconsistent may be the best way to describe Alpha-gal. More than half of us with AGS have had anaphylactic reactions resulting in a visit to the emergency room. Educate your family and friends who may be giving you a ride to the hospital. You'll need an advocate to teach the hospital staff. Most of them have never heard of it. This is not a normal allergy and can't be treated as such. I'm not a doctor and only speaking from my experiences.

Anaphylaxis is a severe allergic reaction and can have many effects on the body.

*Dizziness *faintness *loss of consciousness *anxiety *shock *eye-swelling *itchy mouth *itchy throat *cough *hoarse voice *lips swelling *nasal congestion *difficulty breathing *wheezing, *shortness of breath *low blood pressure * poor circulation *low pulse *chest pain *cramps *nausea *vomiting * diarrhea *itchiness *hives *warmth *redness *rash *pale skin *swelling in hands and feet.

"Are you out of breath just reading that list?"

Listen to your body. Unexplained pain could mean you are unknowingly exposing yourself to mammal.

"Information brings knowledge."

Keep two shots of epinephrine with you at all times. It only works for about twenty minutes. If symptoms return before you reach medical help, another dose may be necessary.

Exercise is good for everyone... *usually.*

It is possible to have exercise induced anaphylaxis. This seems common with AGS patients. Do not exercise right after eating. Stop exercising immediately if you notice any symptoms of anaphylaxis. I have always enjoyed exercising and still do, but I had to change the way I get exercise. If I don't sweat -no reaction. There is a difference in lightly perspiring and actually sweating.

Histamine is a chemical created in the body that is released by white blood cells into the blood stream when the immune system is defending against a potential allergen. While histamine tolerance varies from person to person, avoiding high histamine foods is helpful for Alpha-gal positive people. It is not easy to list all the high histamine foods that could possibly cause issues. If it is fermented, cured, or aged, limit your intake. Stay away from preservatives. Not only are they high in histamines, but could include mammal derived ingredients.

"Make time for your wellness, so you won't have to take time for your illness."

Alpha-gal symptoms and reactions differ from person to person. "The worst case I've seen" is what my allergist said to me. His guess is that I spent too much time without a diagnosis and unknowingly was putting allergens into my body continually. Hosting more hitchhikers (aka ticks!) did not help either. My histamine bucket filled up and overflowed. Multiple symptoms followed including Bell's palsy. I was in the restaurant business handling food daily not realizing the major issues that was causing. Brain fog was so bad that I thought I had a stroke and had been misdiagnosed with Bell's palsy, that was before the AGS diagnosis. We closed the restaurant (a longtime family business) and sold my children's clothing store. My husband continued catering without me. Then I found out I had AGS. It was a tough adjustment with all we had already been through, thankfully I had a lot of support from family and friends. I lost some friends in the process too, but that turned out to be for the best. Some people didn't understand why I couldn't come to their gathering if they were grilling or making things like chili. I had to concentrate on being healthy, my eating habits and lifestyle had to change. A process of mourning my old life had to take place for me to move on.

"Each chapter of life brings new blessings."

- **-Denial**… *no, I can't have a tick disease*
- **-Anger**… *how does a workaholic NOT work?*
- **-Bargaining…** *maybe God allowed this so I can educate people about tick diseases.*
- **-Depression…** *no one cares about tick diseases.*
- **-Acceptance…** *enjoy the little things.*

It took years for me to realize I can still enjoy life -slow learner, I guess. Some people get over AGS and some don't. Concentrate on what you can do instead of what you can't. Open your eyes to a new way of thinking and you'll see wonderful blessings.

Restaurants are challenging with AGS. You must have friends willing to compromise on the selection of restaurants. Always talk to the manager or chef about cross-contamination. If everything is cooked in the same fryer or on the same grill, it is not safe. Places using beef flavoring in their fryers are not safe. Do not be afraid to leave if you don't feel safe. There are establishments willing to accommodate you. Your family and friends love you and would rather change restaurants instead of taking you to the emergency room in a few hours.

"You are not a burden."

Normally, choosing a seafood restaurant is a safe choice. A problem could arise with cross-contamination or dairy. Ask questions for safety, and always emphasize it's an actual allergy -not just an intolerance. If you are a shrimp eater, be aware that some countries inject gelatin into shrimp. **Gelatin** is derived from collagen taken from animal body parts. Education is key. I love Mexican food. Restaurants that serve it became an issue. Fume reactions from those steak fajitas sizzling through the air sent me into an asthma-like reaction. That's when I realized fume reactions were real. I chose to start going to my favorite restaurant between lunch and supper when they don't have a large crowd. The best table was at the back of the bar, far from the kitchen. I could have stopped going but made a decision to keep enjoying their food. They were very accommodating to my needs. Barbecue restaurants with those great smelling smokers can now be a killer if you react to fumes. Vegan restaurants may be a good choice if you're fine with no meat. Carrageenan is an additive sometimes used in vegan products. It has the same molecular structure as Alpha-gal. Highly sensitive people may react to carrageenan. The body can recognize it as Alpha-gal, the enemy.

"I'm literally allergic to bull crap!"

I have often gone into a restaurant with family or friends with the mindset they would have something safe on the menu. That isn't always the case. I cannot tell you how many times I had to eat something from my stash kept in my purse while watching them eat foods I once enjoyed. I try to remind myself I'm there for the company and can handle it. "It's fine, y'all eat." Sometimes I said that on the verge of tears. I started taking an ice chest in my vehicle everywhere I went stocked with a few items that would not make me sick. Some bottled waters even caused reactions. Did you know traces of gelatin can be found in some plastic bottles from companies that use it in their cleansing process? I usually stick with unsweetened tea at restaurants and use organic stevia for sweetener. If you go to a chain restaurant, most have online allergen menus. That helps with dairy allergies but not beef or pork. Finding something labeled vegan is safe most of the time. Unfortunately, it can be trial and error to figure out which restaurants to frequent. Many companies send employees to a class about food allergies and cross-contamination practices. Most people have no idea about AGS or even what animal is actually a mammal.

"There are no mistakes, only lessons."

Anxiety warning… The **BEST** option is to prepare your food in the safety of your own home. It gets old cooking every meal for every day, especially when you don't feel good. Try to prepare more meals on the good days and freeze any leftovers for the not-so-good days. Air fryers and instant pots are great once you learn how to use them. Challenge you family and friends to help discover recipes that are safe for you. Get creative with substitutions to your favorite recipes so they can be Alpha-gal safe. It's a learning process that gets easier as time goes by. My family was in the restaurant business for generations, but there was still a lot of learning involved with this new way of cooking safely. Many stores offer organic items now which helps with shopping. It's best to use organic items whenever possible. Some brands of spices have additives that may not be safe. Sugar is whitened with bone char, mammal of course. Look for organic sugar or one that specifically says 'bone char free' on the packaging. Check ingredient labels often. Some companies change recipes -I don't know why. Living without preservatives is much healthier and safer for everyone. When you look through the included recipes, you'll see how easy substitutions can be.

"No one is born a great cook; one learns by doing."

An **allergy alert bracelet** or necklace can save your life. Make it a priority to order one and always wear it. They can be customized. Mine says: Anaphylaxis, NO gelatin, NO dairy, NO mammal products, Alpha-gal Syndrome.

Keep in mind that medications can contain mammal derived ingredients. My Alpha-gal friends taught me to change from Benadryl to Unisom Sleep Melts. They have the same active ingredient, Diphenhydramine, but with less inactive ingredients such as gelatin. I am convinced that Unisom Sleep Melts have kept me from using my EpiPen many times. They are quick dissolving, non-habit forming and relieve nausea. I never leave home without my EpiPen and Unisom Sleep Melts. Taking one or two melts at the first sign of reaction will usually alleviate symptoms. You may need to lay down afterward, but it beats going to the emergency room. Always talk to your pharmacist about prescription medicine. Chewable baby aspirin works for my headaches. If you require something stronger, check manufacturers for hidden ingredients. Helpful information can be found on social media Alpha-gal pages. People share information they have received from different companies. Robert Woods Johnson Pharmacy at Rutgers University is knowledgeable about Alpha-gal safe meds. They will help you, your doctor or pharmacist.   *Phone number: 732-937-8842*

Tick diseases have become common in the United States and several other countries. Some information can be found on the CDC website about the different types of ticks. You may not find the entire truth on that website. It seems they downplay the seriousness of problems cause by tick diseases. If a person has one tick disease, it is common that another one is hiding in the bloodstream. With any disease, keep track of what your body is telling you. Many tick diseases have similar symptoms. Headaches, fatigue, muscle aches and joint pain are common. A rheumatologist informed me I now have arthritis very likely caused by the tick disease. Yay for me (insert sarcasm)! It's common to have rashes, fever/chills, and sensitivity to the sun. Tanning without turning red and splotchy seems to be over for me. I love the beach but am very cautious about sun exposure now. That's another thing those blood-sucking hitchhikers tried to take from me. I still enjoy the beach for vacations but keep an umbrella nearby. Nasty ticks can't take away my joy of being on vacation with my family. Ticks love me so much that they free-fall from trees just to have a meal with me -on me. Most people with tick diseases love to be outdoors. That's why we get to meet so many of the unwanted guests.

"Ticks are mini, real-life vampires!"

Prevention…

This is something for each person to find out what works for them that DOES NOT cause a reaction. Essential oils have worked well for me. I use a brand named Doterra. There are many brands, and I'm not promoting this one. I had to let you know the brand I use since I'm listing their ingredients.

Tick Repellent

40 drops of Terrashield

10 drops of lemongrass

10 drops of eucalyptus

4 ounces of water

Put into a spray bottle and shake well. Spray onto clothes before enjoying your outdoor activities. I also lightly mist my legs when wearing shorts.

Stores usually stock tick repellents, or you can order online. Always check ingredients for something that may cause a reaction. Once again, the smartest choice will be something labeled vegan. Don't stop camping or enjoying outdoor activities because a blood-sucking creature is lurking.

"Breathe in the fresh air and have fun."

Since having reactions to many medications, I have learned a lot about natural remedies for ailments. Once again, I'm only sharing my experiences. You may not have problems with any of the medicine you are taking. I felt it was too costly to use a compound pharmacy - plus it meant driving to a big city which made me uncomfortable. I love my essential oils. If I have a headache, I put a drop of peppermint on my finger and rub into my temples. Don't get it in your eyes because it will burn.

Anxiety Oil

In a 10 ml roller bottle, add:

10 drops of peppermint

10 drops of lavender

10 drops of frankincense

Add a carrier oil to fill the bottle- I use grapeseed

Rub onto wrist every morning and every evening. The key to this working is being faithful in applying daily. Sometimes I sniff lavender if I feel overwhelmed. It has a calming effect.

Diffusers fill the air with fresh scents. I use different fragrances according to how I feel at the time.
"...1031 references to essential oils in the Bible."

You can order spray bottles and roller bottles online. Amazon is my choice. I don't want to promote them either, but it's a fact. They make it easy to order and receive items quickly.

Did you know that spiders, mice and other vermin hate the smell of peppermint? You can put some on cotton balls and place them around the house. You can also add about 15 drops to a water bottle and spray around the house. That's better than using chemical sprays and taking a chance of having a reaction.

I often add ten drops of peppermint essential oil and ten drops of eucalyptus essential oil to my diffuser. As it flows through the air, I feel like I can breathe deeper. Doterra has created a combination of oils specifically to promote deep breathing. It's simply named Breathe.

Painful Joints Blend

In a 10 ml roller bottle, add:

8 drops of eucalyptus oil

10 drops of peppermint oil

12 drops of lavender oil

Add carrier oil to fill the bottle -olive oil will work

Gently massage painful areas twice a day.

If you do a search for essential oil blends, you will see several choices. I choose the blends that use the least number of oils and then see if it works. This makes the mixing process easier and saves money. There are also blends for better sleep, blood pressure balance, digestive help, and even deodorant. I included the blends I use often for your information. I don't miss my anxiety blend or everyone seems to notice. Having Alpha-gal challenged me to learn about alternative treatments that I have learned to love.

Cannabidiol (CBD) oil is a product that's derived from cannabis. It's a type of cannabinoid, which are the chemicals naturally found in marijuana plants. Even though it comes from marijuana plants, CBD does not create a 'high' effect or any form of intoxication that's caused by another cannabinoid, known as THC. If you're going to try CBD oil, do the research. Find a company that sells a pure form without additives. It may cost a little more but doesn't require as much daily. I am not spending money on prescriptions like I was before, so I feel good about buying CBD oil. When I started taking the pure form every night, the difference was amazing. I have less pain, better sleep, and not as tired during the day. Exhaustion from accidental exposure went from three days to only one day.
"Health is not valued until sickness comes."

Acupuncture is a form of alternative medicine. Even though it is controversial, I want to give as much information as I can from my experiences. I have had one treatment at this point -a life-changing treatment. While there is no cure for Alpha-gal, some people have improved using Soliman's Auricular Allergy Treatment better known as SAAT. It is said to 'reprogram' your immune system to stop over reacting to allergens. Dr. Nader Soliman, a pioneer in auricular acupuncture, completed years of clinical study on thousands of allergy sufferers. Through his refined method of SAAT, individuals now experience severe reduction and even elimination of allergy symptoms. This treatment is being used on AGS patients with some success. After one treatment (a tiny needle placed strategically in the ear for three weeks), I can eat cheese without any pain or reaction. My goal -to be able to have cheese again and do better with cross contamination. That was accomplished along with less fume reactions. I have had anaphylaxis too many times to ever want red meats again, but some people have had success with that too. I began to feel half-way normal again. After some ticks fell out of trees while I was picnicking -and of course had a picnic with my blood, some cross contamination issues returned. I look forward to another SAAT visit.

"Acupuncture is a jab well done."

When cooking at home…

Alpha-gal friendly foods can be substituted in many recipes to make safe and enjoyable meals. Buying fresh foods is best but not always possible. When buying canned products, make sure they are organic. Frozen vegetables usually have no additives which makes them safe. Packaged meats can have preservatives, so try to choose the ones with few ingredients and NO preservatives. Some companies add fillers to spices - always check them for those unwanted additives. I understand it's sometimes difficult to find organic foods in small towns. I try to use simple ingredients and stock up when I find canned organic vegetables. I have created recipes or received them from friends and online. Once you realize what you can substitute, you'll see most recipes can be adjusted. Measuring is not fun for me since I go by taste as I add spices. The following recipes may need to be tweaked to your taste. After having Bell's palsy four times, sometimes I have a problem tasting salt. After eliminating all mammal, no more Bell's palsy but permanent damage was done. Dysfunctional vocal cord and synkinesis cause some issues -still living and enjoying life though.

"The secret of change is to focus all your energy, not on fighting the old, but on building the new." Socrates

Substitutions:

1 tbsp cornstarch = *2 tbsp unbleached flour*

1 cup buttermilk =*add 1 tbsp vinegar to 1 c. almond milk*

1 cup cream, sour or heavy = *⅓ cup plant butter with ⅔ cup non-dairy milk*

1 tbsp minced onion = *1 small fresh onion*

⅛ tsp garlic powder = *1 small pressed clove of garlic*

3 medium bananas = *1 cup mashed*

Butter = *plant butter*

Milk = *non-dairy milk*

Flour = *unbleached flour or almond flour for gluten-free*

Ketchup = *organic ketchup*

Chocolate = *non-dairy dark chocolate (look for Enjoy Life products)*

Sugar = *organic or bone-char free sugar; stevia*

Bacon = *turkey bacon or chicken bacon*

Pork sausage = *duck or turkey sausage*

Cheeses = *non-dairy options or nutritional yeast*

"Invest in a meat thermometer for safety."

Appetizers And Dips

Vegan Cheese Sauce

- *½ cup nutritional yeast*
- *⅓ cup all-purpose unbleached flour*
- *1 tsp sea salt*
- *2 cups cold water*
- *¼ cup plant butter*
- *1 tsp mustard*

Whisk together nutritional yeast, unbleached flour, and sea salt in a pan. Put on stove top, medium heat and whisk in the water. Bring to a boil, reduce heat and cook for 1 minute. Continue whisking to keep it from sticking to the pan. Remove from heat and stir in plant butter and mustard. This makes a great cheesy tasting sauce to pour over dishes that require cheese. If too thin, add flour. If too thick, add 1 tbsp water or almond milk.

To make into **cheese dip**, add ½ tbsp garlic powder and 1 tbsp chili powder. More salt and chopped jalapenos are optional.

"Smile and say CHEESE please."

Notes

Homemade Salsa

- *15 ounce can organic petite diced tomatoes or use 3 fresh medium sized tomatoes and chop to petite size*
- *1 cup finely chopped chili peppers*
- *½ cup finely chopped onions*
- *1 tsp garlic powder*
- *½ tsp cumin*
- *½ tsp bone-char free sugar*
- *½ tsp sea salt*
- *1 finely chopped jalapeno (optional)*

Mix all ingredients together in a large bowl and use a mixer to blend. You can use a food processor or blender, but be careful not to over-blend if you like the chunky kind of salsa. Serve with chips and enjoy!

*Tomatoes are high in histamine so avoid if you've had an allergic reaction recently.

"Salsa… a snack or a dance. Why not choose both?"

Notes

Carrot Dip

- *4 medium carrots*
- *2 tbsp olive oil*
- *½ tsp sea salt*
- *3 tsp sesame seeds*
- *½ tsp black pepper*
- *1 garlic clove*
- *½ cup water*

Peel and clean carrots, boil until soft. Cut into 1" pieces. In a food processor or by hand, grind carrots adding all ingredients until you have a paste-like consistency. Serve at room temperature with pita chips.

"Carrots have been linked to lower cholesterol and improved eye health."

Notes

Paleo Sausage Balls

- *1 lb duck or turkey sausage*
- *1 cup plus 2 tbsp almond flour*
- *3 tbsp tapioca starch*
- *3 tbsp nutritional yeast*
- *1 tsp sea salt*
- *¼ tsp black pepper*
- *2 tsp thyme leaves*
- *1 tsp ground sage*
- *2 eggs*
- *¼ tsp cayenne (optional)*

Preheat oven 400° F. Line baking sheet with parchment paper. In a large mixing bowl, combine sausage, flour, starch, yeast and seasonings. Fold in eggs, stir well until fully combined. Scoop out small balls shaping them with your hands. Place on baking sheet evenly spaced. Bake 30 to 35 minutes or until fully cooked.

"Paleo recipes mean Alpha-gal safe? -Not always."

Notes

Black Bean Dip

- *2 tsp grape seed oil (canola or olive oil works too)*
- *½ medium onion, finely chopped*
- *1 tsp oregano*
- *½ tsp cumin*
- *Pinch of cayenne*
- *15 ounce can organic black beans, drained but save juice*
- *½ tsp sea salt*
- *Juice from ½ lime*
- *Cilantro for garnish*

Heat oil over medium heat in sauté pan. Add onions, oregano and cook until onions start to turn brown. Add cumin and cayenne, cook 1 minute. Add beans and cook for 3 minutes. Remove from heat and puree' until desired smoothness is reached. Add bean juice 1 tsp at a time if the dip is too stiff. Stir in salt and lime juice. Check for flavor and add salt or other spices as needed to fit your taste. Serve warm with tortilla chips.

You can sprinkle vegan shredded cheese on top or stir in some nutritional yeast for a slight cheesy flavor.

"I love cheesy bean dip."

Notes

Avocado Dip

- *2 ripe avocados*
- *½ tsp garlic powder*
- *¼ tsp sea salt*
- *⅛ tsp black pepper*
- *¼ onion finely chopped*
- *¼ chopped tomato (optional)*
- *1 lime*

Peel the avocados and remove seed. Place into a bowl, add garlic powder, salt, pepper, onion, and tomato. Gently mash all ingredients together. Stir in the lime juice and it's ready to eat. Serve with chips or use for a topping on your favorite Mexican dish.

Make a salad and use this for your dressing. You can thin the avocado dip by mixing in 1 tbsp melted plant butter and 1 tbsp non-dairy milk.

"Avocados are full of healthy, beneficial fats that help you feel full and satisfied."

Notes

Artichoke Dip

- *8 ounces artichokes cut up*
- *1 cup mayonnaise (I prefer Dukes)*
- *¼ tsp garlic powder (2 cloves garlic)*
- *1 cup shredded vegan parmesan cheese*

Preheat oven to 350° F. Mix together all ingredients. Bake for 25 minutes. Serve with tortilla chips or pita chips.

"Artichokes are known as being a superfood because of their high levels of antioxidants. Studies show they help balance blood pressure, lower cholesterol and can improve liver function."

↑That's amazing!

Notes

Cowboy Caviar

- *15 ounce can of black-eyed peas, drained (another option is to cook a bag of frozen black-eyed peas, cooked and cooled)*
- *15 ounce can of corn, drained (optional to use frozen bag of corn)*
- *1 ¾ cup olive oil*
- *¾ cup vinegar*
- *1 small onion, finely chopped*
- *½ cup diced tomatoes*
- *¼ cup diced jalapenos*
- *1 tbsp garlic powder*
- *1 tbsp oregano*
- *1 tbsp crushed red pepper*
- *2 tsp lemon juice*

Mix seasonings and liquids, shake well. Add to the remaining ingredients and stir. Chill and serve with chips or crackers.

"This is good served as a side salad too."

Notes

Veggie Dip

- *24 ounces roasted red peppers*
- *½ tsp garlic powder*
- *2 tsp mustard*
- *⅛ tsp sea salt*
- *⅛ tsp black pepper*
- *1 medium yellow pepper, diced*
- *1 tbsp ginger root, minced*
- *¼ cup basil (fresh) chopped*

Use a blender or food processor, combine roasted peppers, garlic, ginger root and mustard. Puree' until smooth. Season to taste with salt and pepper. Transfer to a large bowl and fold in remaining ingredients.

***Homemade roasted peppers** *-preheat oven to 450° F. Cut the peppers in half, remove stems, seeds and membranes. Lay the peppers on a foil-lined baking sheet cut side down. Roast the peppers for 15-20 minutes or until skins are dark and have collapsed. Remove from oven. Skin should come off easily at this point. Discard skin, chop, dice or freeze for use.*

"Homemade is the best!"

Notes

Soups & Salads

Banana Apple Salad

- *⅓ cup honey*
- *½ tsp lemon zest*
- *3 tbsp lemon juice*
- *¼ tsp sea salt*
- *1 tsp ground ginger*
- *⅛ tsp nutmeg*
- *1 lb bananas, cut into ½ inch slices*
- *1 lb apples, cut into ½ inch chunks*
- *Chopped nuts (optional)*

In a large bowl, whisk together honey, zest, juice, salt, ginger and nutmeg. Add bananas and apples, toss and serve.

"A refreshing summer side or lunch."

Notes

English Pea Salad

- *15 ounces cooked sweet green peas*
- *½ medium onion, finely chopped*
- *2 boiled eggs, chopped*
- *1 cup sweet pickles, chopped*
- *½ tsp sea salt*
- *¼ tsp black pepper*
- *2 green onions, chopped*
- *½ cup mayonnaise (Dukes is my choice)*

Let the peas cool. Put all ingredients in a bowl and mix well. Chill for at least one hour before serving.

"Try it… if you like it, make it for friends and family. People will be asking for your recipe."

Notes

Broccoli Salad

- *1 head broccoli*
- *1 small bag shredded carrots*
- *½ cup raisins*
- *1 cup mayonnaise (prefer Dukes)*
- *¼ cup bone-char free sugar*
- *2 tbsp vinegar*
- *½ cup chopped red onions*
- *¼ cup chopped walnuts*
- *¼ cup chopped pineapple (optional)*

Cut broccoli into bite sized pieces and put in a large bowl. Add carrots, raisins, mayo, sugar, vinegar, and onions. Mix well. Top with walnuts and enjoy.

*I only use organic fruits and nuts. It is healthier to stay away from preservatives and pesticides. My throat got itchy, and I would cough before switching to organic only.

"Broccoli… packed with vitamins and does a body good."

Notes

Chicken Salad

- *2 cooked chicken breasts, diced*
- *¼ cup mayonnaise (can add more according to your taste)*
- *1 small peeled and chopped organic apple*
- *¼ onion, chopped (optional)*
- *¼ cup chopped grapes*
- *Splash of lemon juice*
- *½ tsp mustard*
- *Sea salt and pepper to taste*

Mix all ingredients together in a medium sized bowl.

Dip- *serve with Alpha-gal safe crackers*

Sandwich- *layer on bread (I use Dave's Killer Bread), add lettuce and tomato*

Wrap- *put on a tortilla with a leaf of lettuce*

Salad- *place on top of a bed of greens such as romaine and spinach*

Lettuce Wrap- *roll in a romaine lettuce leaf*

"Happiness is having good food to take to the picnic."

Notes

Macaroni Salad

- *1 cup uncooked elbow macaroni*
- *½ cup mayonnaise*
- *2 hardboiled eggs, chopped*
- *1 green pepper, chopped*
- *1 cucumber, chopped*
- *1 medium onion, chopped*

Cook elbow macaroni as directed on the package. Drain and add remaining ingredients. Stir lightly and chill.

"Pasta salads are a great addition to cookouts."

Notes

Pasta e Fagiolo Soup

- *1 tbsp olive oil*
- *1 lb ground chicken or ground turkey*
- *2 organic carrots, diced*
- *2 stalks organic celery, diced*
- *1 medium onion, diced*
- *28 ounces crushed tomatoes (prefer organic)*
- *2 bay leaves*
- *1 tbsp oregano*
- *½ tsp thyme*
- *1 tsp sea salt*
- *½ tsp black pepper*
- *2 cans white or pinto beans (or make them from scratch)*
- *1 cup elbow macaroni*

Add oil, onion and meat to large pot and brown. Add other ingredients except pasta. Simmer on stove at least one hour. Cook pasta according to the package and add to soup.

*Crock pot- brown meat the same but add to crock pot with ingredients except pasta. High for 3 hours. Low for 6 hours. Add pasta for the last thirty minutes to allow time for it to cook in the crock pot.

Notes

Chicken Summer Stew

- *2 boneless chicken breasts*
- *1 tsp sea salt*
- *½ tsp black pepper*
- *1 tbsp unbleached flour*
- *2 tbsp olive oil*
- *1 ½ cups yellow corn*
- *3 tbsp plant butter*
- *1 yellow squash, sliced thinly*
- *1 small zucchini, sliced thinly*
- *10 ounces frozen baby lima beans, thawed*
- *3 ripe plum tomatoes, seeded and cut into ⅓ inch dice*
- *4 cups organic chicken broth*
- *¼ cup fresh chives- ½ inch length*

Season chicken with salt and pepper. Sprinkle with flour. Heat olive oil in a 2 ½ quart pan over medium heat. Add chicken; cook covered until chicken is done. Remove from heat, place chicken on a board to cool. Melt butter in pan; add squash, zucchini, lima beans, and corn. Cook, stirring often, until squash is wilted for about 4-5 minutes. Cut chicken into ¾ inch chunks. Add to vegetables plus tomatoes and broth. Season with salt and pepper. Cook until heated through- 3 to 4 minutes. Sprinkle chives on top before serving.

Notes

Homemade Chili

- *1 lb ground chicken or ground turkey*
- *1 tbsp olive oil*
- *1 small onion chopped*
- *1 tsp sea salt*
- *½ black pepper*
- *1 tbsp garlic powder*
- *2 tbsp chili powder*
- *Add 3 cans tri-blend organic beans or use homemade pinto beans*
- *1 can organic tomato sauce*
- *1 tbsp bone-char free sugar*

In a large pot, add oil, meat and chopped onion. As the meat browns, stir in the salt, pepper, garlic and chili powder. Once the meat is done, add beans, tomato sauce and sugar. Simmer for 30 minutes to an hour, adding water if too thick. Add more seasonings according to your taste.

"Chill out and enjoy that chili!"

Notes

Chicken Veggie Soup

- *1 lb ground chicken or ground turkey*
- *1 tbsp olive oil*
- *½ onion, chopped*
- *16 ounces (one bag) frozen vegetable*
- *2 potatoes, cleaned and cut in 1-inch chunks*
- *1 can organic petite diced tomatoes or wash and dice one small tomato*
- *1 lb organic chicken bone broth*
- *2 tsp sea salt*
- *1 tsp black pepper*
- *½ tbsp garlic powder*
- *1 tbsp oregano*

Add oil, onion and meat to a large pot. As the meat browns, add sea salt, pepper, garlic and oregano. When the meat is done, add bone broth, frozen vegetables, potatoes, and diced tomatoes. Bring to a boil, then lower heat to simmer for about 30-45 minutes. More broth or water can be added if you prefer thinner soup.

"Do your squats, eat your veggies and be kind."

Notes

Main Dishes

Meatloaf Stuffed Bell Peppers

- *1 lb ground chicken or ground turkey*
- *¼ cup crushed crackers*
- *¼ cup organic ketchup (plus 4 tbsp optional)*
- *1 egg, beaten*
- *1 tsp onion powder*
- *1 tsp garlic powder*
- *1 tsp sea salt*
- *½ tsp black pepper*
- *4 bell peppers with tops removed and seeds discarded (when choosing peppers, look for the ones with the flattest bottom.)*

Preheat oven 350° F. In a large mixing bowl, combine the meat, crackers, ¼ cup of ketchup, egg, onion powder, garlic powder, salt and pepper. Mix thoroughly. Divide the meat mixture evenly among the peppers. Bake for 50 minutes. Take out of oven and add a tbsp of ketchup on each one. This step can be skipped if you prefer meatloaf without topping. Put back into oven for another 10 minutes. Use a meat thermometer to make sure the internal temperature has reached 165° F. Cool slightly and serve.

"Meatloaf with ketchup is yummy, but 'good gravy' works too"

Notes

Turkey Tenderloin

- *2 lb package of turkey tenderloins (there should be 2 in the package)*
- *2 tbsp olive oil*
- *1 tsp sea salt*
- *2 tbsp oregano*
- *½ tsp mustard*
- *1 tbsp thyme (optional)*
- *½ tsp black pepper*
- *1 tbsp garlic powder*

Preheat oven to 400° F. Place turkey tenderloin in an oven safe pan with sides -lining the pan with foil will save on clean-up. Score tenderloins across the top with a knife, so the oil and seasonings can seep into the meat. Place a tbsp of oil on each loin. Rub spices into each tenderloin. Cover with foil and bake for approximately one hour. Remove the foil covering the loins and check for internal temperature of 165°. Over cooking can cause the meat to be dry, so you may want to check them about ¾ way through cooking time. Let the loins cool for about 10 minutes prior to slicing. These are similar to pork loins but no pork.

"Let's talk turkey."

Notes

Barbeque Chicken

- *4- 4 ounce boneless chicken breasts, dark meat can be used with a little added cooking time*
- *8 ounces organic barbeque sauce*

Instant Pot- Lay the chicken breasts in the pot. Cover chicken with barbeque sauce, seal the lid. Use the 'meat' button and cook for 28 minutes. After releasing the air, open and shred the meat using two forks. Serve

Crock Pot- Put the chicken breasts in the crock pot, cover with sauce. Cook on high for 2 hours or low for 4 hours. Shred the chicken and serve.

BBQ chicken can be served on buns (I use Dave's Killer Bread). Extra sauce can be added according to your taste. Making BBQ spuds is another option. Just bake a potato, add a tbsp of plant butter, chicken, more sauce if desired and shredded vegan cheese.

Homemade Barbeque Sauce

- *8 ounces organic ketchup*
- *2 tsp chili powder*
- *2 tsp garlic powder*
- *1 tsp onion powder*
- *2 tsp organic sugar*

Mix all ingredients and adjust to your taste.

"Happiness is homemade."

Notes

Taco Meat

- *1 lb ground chicken or ground turkey*
- *1 small onion, chopped*
- *½ tbsp garlic powder*
- *1 tbsp chili powder*
- *1 tsp sea salt*
- *½ tsp black pepper*
- *1 tbsp olive oil*
- *¼ cup of water*

Add oil, meat and chopped onions to skillet. Turn to medium heat, add all other ingredients except the water. When meat looks done, turn down to a simmer and add water. Let simmer until the water has boiled down. Taste to see if you prefer more spices. I often add a little extra chili powder and garlic. It only needs to simmer on low for about ten minutes, making a quick and easy meal.

*Add to taco shells, top with lettuce, vegan cheese and tomatoes. Use a flour tortilla for soft tacos. *Put on a bed of lettuce for a taco salad, top with organic salsa. *Spread some tortilla chips on a plate, add taco meat, lettuce and vegan cheese. (Vegan cheese sauce is good with this also.)

"Taco seasoning blend can be made ahead and kept in shaker or sealed in a baggie. Substitute 1 tsp onion powder in place of the small onion. I like real onions for the aroma while cooking."

Notes

Apple Turkey Chops

- *4 turkey breast cutlets*
- *2 medium apples, peeled, cored and sliced*
- *2 tsp plant butter*
- *¼ tsp cinnamon (optional)*
- *Sea salt and pepper to taste*

Preheat oven to 350° F. Salt and pepper cutlets on both sides. Brown the cutlets in a skillet. Place browned culets in lightly greased baking dish. Layer apples on top of cutlets. Dot with plant butter and sprinkle with cinnamon. Cover and bake until apples and cutlets are done. Check after 20 minutes to see if internal temperature has reached 165° F. Ovens vary, and may need extra cooking time.

"TALK TURKEY-

the origin of this phrase seems to come from colonial times. Historical accounts suggest the phrase came about from the day-to-day bartering over wild turkeys."

Notes

Lemon Baked Chicken

- *4 boneless skinless chicken breasts (dark meat can be used with added cooking time*
- *¼ cup plus 2 tbsp lemon juice*
- *½ cup melted plant butter*
- *1 tsp garlic*
- *1 tsp oregano*
- *1 tsp sea salt*
- *½ tsp black pepper*

Preheat oven to 350° F. Place chicken in a lightly greased baking dish. Combine all ingredients, pour over chicken, bake covered for 30 minutes. Remove from oven. Uncover and spoon juices over the chicken. Return to oven for another 15 minutes. Remove from oven and check internal temperature. It should be at least 165° F. Bake longer if the temperature has not reached that point. Baking times vary according to the size of the chicken breasts.

"Chicken or egg- which came first?"

Notes

Smothered Chicken

- *4 boneless skinless chicken breasts*
- *½ cup unbleached flour*
- *2 tbsp olive oil*
- *½ onion, chopped*
- *½ tbsp chili powder*
- *½ tbsp garlic powder*
- *1 tsp sea salt*
- *½ tsp black pepper*

In a deep skillet add olive oil and chopped onion, put on medium heat on stove. Add the spices to the flour and spread out on a plate. Flour the chicken breasts on both sides and add to the skillet. Make sure you can visibly see the oil in the skillet. If not, add an extra tbsp. The remaining flour left on the plate can now be added to the skillet as well. Try to put it around the chicken into the oil. Cook chicken on one side for about 5 minutes, then flip to the other side for another 5 minutes. Then add water to just cover the chicken. Let it come to a boil, then cover and simmer for about 30 minutes, stirring the gravy around chicken occasionally. Check the gravy for taste and add more seasonings as needed for your preference. The chicken should be tender at this point. Add more water if the gravy is too thick. If it's thin, you may want to let it simmer a little longer.

Notes

Spaghetti Meat Sauce

- *1 lb ground chicken or ground turkey*
- *½ onion, chopped*
- *1 tbsp olive oil*
- *1 can organic tomato sauce*
- *1 can organic petite diced tomatoes*
- *½ tbsp garlic powder*
- *1 tbsp oregano*
- *1 tsp sea salt*
- *½ tsp black pepper*
- *1 tbsp bone-char free sugar*

In a deep skillet, add olive oil, onion and meat. Cook over medium heat until done. Add all remaining ingredients. Bring the sauce to a boil, then simmer for 20-30 minutes, stirring occasionally. My family likes a little extra garlic and oregano, but always season to your preferred taste. It can be thinned by adding water.

When buying pasta, check the ingredients on the package for added preservatives. Try to buy pasta with the least amount of ingredients. I like to buy organic, but it's not always easy to find.

"I was in a supermarket and saw Paul Newman's face on salad dressing and spaghetti sauce... I thought he was missing."　　　　　*-Bob Saget*

Notes

Mexican Lasagna

- *1 lb ground chicken or ground turkey*
- *1 small onion chopped*
- *2 tbsp olive oil*
- *1 tbsp garlic powder*
- *1 ½ tbsp chili powder*
- *1 tsp sea salt*
- *½ tsp black pepper*
- *12 corn tortillas*
- *1 can organic corn, drained (frozen can be used)*
- *1 can organic tri-blend beans (homemade pinto beans can be used instead)*
- *1 can organic petite diced tomatoes*
- *6 ounces shredded vegan cheese or vegan cheese sauce*

Preheat oven to 350° F.

In a deep skillet, add 1 tbsp olive oil and chopped onion to meat. Brown meat mixing the onions into the meat. Add garlic, chili powder. Salt and pepper. Stir in corn, beans and tomatoes. Bring to a boil, then remove from heat. In a baking dish, spread 1 tbsp oil on bottom. Layer 6 corn tortillas in the bottom. Scoop half the meat mixture onto the tortillas. Layer the other 6 tortillas, then add the rest of the meat mixture. Put shredded cheese or cheese sauce on top. Bake for 30-40 minutes. Remove from oven, let cool slightly before cutting.

"Is it Mexican or Italian? …a little more Mexican I think."

Notes

Sweets

And

Other

Things

Old Fashioned Homemade Biscuits

- *2 cups unbleached all purpose flour (make it gluten-free by substituting almond flour)*
- *2 ½ tsp baking powder (most brands are safe, but always check ingredients label)*
- *½ tsp sea salt*
- *⅓ cup all vegetable shortening*
- *¾ cup unsweetened almond milk*
- *1 tbsp softened plant butter*

Preheat oven to 475° F. In a medium mixing bowl stir together flour, baking powder and salt. Cut in shortening until it resembles coarse crumbs. (A pastry blender makes it easier but not necessary.) Make a well in the center of the flour mixture. Add milk. Using a fork, stir until moistened and dough pulls away from the sides of the bowl (dough will be sticky). On a floured surface, lightly knead dough with floured hands until nearly smooth. Roll dough to ¾ inch thickness. Cut dough with a 2 ½ inch biscuit cutter (I use a glass) dipping cutter into flour between cuts. Place biscuits close together on a lightly greased baking sheet. Brush tops with soft butter. Bake 12-15 minutes or until center is done. Yields about 8 biscuits. Add plant butter, honey or an all-fruit jelly. (Thanks sister Vicky for teaching me.)

"Practice makes perfect."

Notes

Chocolate Gravy

- *¾ cup bone-char free sugar*
- *½ cup unbleached all-purpose flour*
- *⅓ cup cocoa*
- *3 cups unsweetened almond milk*
- *1 tsp vanilla*
- *½ stick plant butter*
- *½ cup warm water*

Mix dry ingredients together. Add warm water and stir well. Heat almond milk in saucepan until almost boiling. Pour the hot almond milk into the cocoa mixture, stirring constantly until it starts to thicken. Add plant butter and vanilla. The key is stirring constantly, and it will turn out great. How about having this with those old-fashioned homemade biscuits.

"Chocolate comes from cocoa which is a tree. That makes it a plant. Chocolate is salad."

Notes

Apple Crisp

- *4 cups peeled and slice apples*
- *1 tsp cinnamon*
- *¼ to ½ tsp sea salt*
- *¾ cup unbleached all-purpose flour*
- *¼ cup water*
- *1 cup bone-char free sugar*
- *⅓ cup plant butter*

Preheat oven to 350° F.

Spread apples in buttered baking dish. Sprinkle with cinnamon and salt. Add water evenly to apples (do not stir). Mix together flour, sugar, and butter until mixture looks crumbly. Drop mixture over apples. Bake for 40 minutes. Serve warm.

"Fruit as a dessert… yum."

Notes

Microwave Mug Cake

- *¼ cup unbleached all-purpose flour*
- *¼ cup bone-char free sugar*
- *2 tbsp cocoa powder*
- *Pinch of salt*
- *Pinch of baking soda*
- *1 tbsp water*
- *2 tbsp olive oil*
- *3 tbsp unsweetened almond milk*
- *A splash of vanilla*

In a large coffee mug, put all the dry ingredients and stir. Then add water, oil, milk and vanilla. Stir well. Microwave for 2 minutes. Then let cool for 2 minutes.

This is very sweet, but if you really have a sweet tooth… you can poke holes in it and pour chocolate syrup over it. There's one chocolate syrup that says 'Simply Five' on it and only contains five ingredients.

"This mug cake serves one person and is a special treat."

Notes

Sugar Cookies

- *1 cup plant butter*
- *1 cup bone-char free sugar*
- *1 large egg*
- *1 tbsp vanilla*
- *¼ tsp almond extract (optional)*
- *2 ½ cups unbleached all-purpose flour*
- *½ tsp baking soda*
- *½ tsp baking powder*

Topping: ½ cup bone-char free sugar, for rolling cookie dough balls

Preheat oven to 350° F.

In a large mixing bowl, cream together butter and sugar until light and fluffy. Add egg, extracts, and mix until smooth. Add flour, baking powder, baking soda, and mix until just combined to a cookie dough consistency. Scoop out small portions of the dough and make balls. Roll in the sugar (topping). Place them on a cookie sheet, lined with parchment paper. Bake for 12 minutes or until edges are lightly golden. Allow to cool and enjoy!

"This is my husband's favorite!"

Notes

Peanut Butter Fudge

- *3 ½ cups organic powdered sugar*
- *1 stick plant butter*
- *½ cup peanut butter (Earth Balance is my choice)*
- *¼ cup unsweetened almond milk*
- *1 tsp vanilla*

Pour sugar into large microwave safe bowl. Add butter, milk and peanut butter. Do not stir. Place in microwave oven for 2 ½ minutes or until butter melts. Take bowl out of microwave, add vanilla and mix with electric mixer. Pour into an 8 x 8-inch baking dish that has been lined with foil. Place in freezer for 15 minutes.

Sometimes humidity causes issues with thickening. This is still delicious even if it doesn't make a thick fudge.

"Throw in some dairy-free chocolate chips, and it's the perfect dessert for me."

Notes

Hot Cocoa

- *¼ cup cocoa*
- *½ cup bone-char free sugar*
- *Dash of sea salt*
- *⅓ cup hot water*
- *1 quart (32 ounces) unsweetened almond milk*
- *¾ tsp vanilla*

Add cocoa, sugar, salt and hot water to a pot. Bring to a boil and stir for 2 minutes. Add milk. Stir and heat. DO NOT BOIL. Remove from heat and add ¾ tsp vanilla. Whisk or use mixer until foamy. Put into mugs and enjoy!

You can add vegan marshmallows or dairy-free whipped cream to the top.

"This will warm you up on a cool evening."

Notes

Best Vegan Brownies

- *2 tbsp ground flaxseed*
- *6 tbsp water or chilled brewed coffee*
- *1 cup dairy-free chocolate chips, melted*
- *1 cup bone-char free sugar*
- *6 tbsp plant butter*
- *1 tsp vanilla*
- *¾ cup + 2 tbsp unbleached all-purpose flour (can substitute gluten-free flour)*
- *1 tsp sea salt*
- *1 tsp baking powder*
- *¼ cup cocoa powder*
- *1 ½ cups dairy-free chocolate chips*

Preheat oven to 350° F. Combine flaxseed and water (or coffee). Let it sit for 10 minutes, to form a gel. Line a square pan with parchment paper and set aside. In a large mixing bowl, add butter and sugar, whisk well. Add in the flaxseed mixture, melted chocolate, vanilla and mix well, until glossy. Now stir in flour, baking powder, salt and cocoa powder until combined. Do not overmix. Fold in the 1 ½ cups of chocolate chips. Transfer brownie batter into the lined pan. Bake for 30-35 minutes. Remove brownies from oven and cool completely before slicing into 12 pieces. You will not be able to tell these are vegan. They are delicious.

Notes

Microwave Burger Bun

- *3 tbsp almond flour or unbleached all-purpose flour*
- *½ tsp baking powder*
- *1 ½ tbsp olive oil*
- *1 egg*
- *Pinch of sea salt*
- *Pinch of nutritional yeast flakes*

In a small cereal bowl (microwave-safe bowl), thoroughly mix the baking powder and flour ensuring there are no clumps. Add the oil, egg, salt and yeast, mix well. Using a fork, make sure it is mixed well with no clumps. Microwave on high for 90 seconds. When you take out of the microwave, the bun will be in the shape of the bottom of the bowl. Let it cool before slicing. This can be toasted for turkey burgers or emu burgers. It can also be used for egg sandwiches or just as a bun with your meal.

This recipe makes one serving.

"Turkey burgers are enjoyable, but emu burgers remind me of those old-fashioned beef burgers."

Notes

There are many more recipes I could have included. Here are some hints.

In place of beef, use **emu** meat. The ground emu is best with duck fat as it is very lean meat. Emu rump can be used in place of beef roast. Emu filets will make good steaks, cooked as you did beef steaks.

Remember your favorite pork chop recipes? Replace pork chops with **turkey cutlets.** They can be grilled, smothered with gravy, fried or baked. Pork loin recipes can still be followed simply by substituting turkey tenderloin.

Any ground beef recipe can be followed by substituting ground **turkey**, ground **chicken** or ground **emu**. Add 1 tbsp oil per pound of ground meat.

Turkey bacon can be used in place of pork bacon for cooking. When making a 'bacon' sandwich or an egg and bacon sandwich, I use Al Fresco uncured **chicken bacon** fully cooked. I also add it to green beans for flavor. The fully cooked chicken bacon (2 pieces) can be put into microwave for 20 seconds, let set a few minutes for crispness.

Although I didn't include any fish recipes, we often eat grilled fish.

FISH

For fish about 2 inches thick, season with your favorite spices. Be sure the grill is clean. Apply some olive oil to a paper towel. Using tongs, rub the oil covered paper towel along the grates. Let the temperature of the grill heat up between 550° to 600° F. Lay the fish skin side down onto the grate. Do not try to move or flip fish until seared good on the side down on the grill. Cook about 6 minutes on one side lid down, then turn for about 6 minutes on the other side with lid down. The fish should turn out flaky and delicious.

Fish wrapped in foil and grilled is also easy and tastes great. Lay the fish in the middle of the foil, add desired spices and a drizzle of olive oil. Add a slice of lemon on each one. Fold up edges of foil so that it's completely sealed, creating a tent. (I have also added sliced squash or zucchini on the top of the fish to cook along with the fish.) It's best to cook foil wrapped foods on indirect heat, meaning do not put on direct flame. Heat half the grill at high heat. Put the foil packets on the other half, close grill and cook about 15 minutes. The steam created inside the foil tent cooks this meal to perfection. Adjust cooking time according to the thickness of the fish. Foil packets can be steamed in a 400° oven if weather isn't good for grilling outside.

Things I learned the hard way...

Who would have thought alpha-gal would still be present on mammal products if the animal is dead?

Do not lick an envelope to seal it. Symptoms for me were immediate with tongue getting numb and swelling. The envelopes that seal without licking them are the best choice.

Check your bandages before applying to your skin. The stickiness can be mammal based causing redness and a rash. Difficulty breathing was also one of my symptoms.

Monitor leads from a heart monitor ended up in painful burning after being on the skin for about an hour. The skin under the leads was red with small blisters. The solution was using leads for sensitive skin. Be sure to ask for these if you need to go to the hospital or emergency room.

Scotch tape... they make a plant-based tape now.

Suede boots worn over socks and leggings... this I couldn't believe and wore them a second time. That proved the first time wasn't just a fluke. My feet and legs up to the top of the boot line itched badly and turned red. No more suede boots for me. Some complain about leather furniture but I haven't experienced that.

My head itched for about three weeks. I finally asked a friend to look at my scalp. She was shocked to see it was covered with red marks and appeared as though someone had clawed my head all over. I immediately changed to a certified vegan shampoo. Healing began and problem solved.

Face moisturizer was advertised as vegan. I bought it and tried it. My face and neck became hot and red. I started sweating also. I looked at the container. It didn't have a certified vegan symbol anywhere. Although it was advertised as vegan, it was not.

Hotel sheets can be washed in any kind of detergent. After experiencing rash and difficulty breathing, we only travel in our own camper with all my safe items.

Ant bites now cause anaphylaxis. I stepped in a bed of ants and received several bites on my foot and ankle. Immediately itchiness, redness and swelling started. Within a couple of hours, I had brain fog, exhaustion, blood pressure drop and nausea. Symptoms were continually getting worse, so I took Unisom Sleep Melts and laid down. After sleeping for about ten hours, I woke up to bumps and itchiness where the bites were and still felt very tired. The other symptoms were better, but it was very tough functioning that day (which was the day after the bites).

Others have reported being allergic to bee and/or wasp stings after the diagnosis of Alpha-gal. Thankfully, I have not been stung. After further study, it seems ants and bees are genetically related. Since I know ant bites cause a reaction, it makes sense that bees would too.

Driving or riding in a car. Suddenly there's that dead skunk smell. Without even realizing a reaction could occur from that, I went into an asthma attack. This happened on more than one occasion. *ALWAYS* keep your air conditioning vents on inside air. It may not stop all possible fume reactions out but will help.

Ice cream made with almond milk caused reactions three times before I realized it contained carrageenan. *Vegan does not always mean safe.*

Deodorant can be bad, causing underarm rash and burning. Look for a vegan deodorant that will work for you. Everyone is different on this one.

I had to replace my toothpaste. Oh my, and the toothbrush with tongue cleaner on the back made me feel like I had been eating razor blades.

Be careful about using razor blades with lanolin. There's nothing like burning pain all over the shaved areas. I used *organic* coconut oil to help. The regular coconut oil made it worse!

A message from my husband...

"Alpha-gal is serious. Always be an advocate for your loved one and believe they are hurting and possibly depressed. Life may have to change for the entire family and that's ok. Family and friends need to accept things are different in order to help. This can get serious fast. What may not cause a reaction one time will be anaphylaxis the next time. I saw her up in the middle of the night vomiting more times than you can imagine. Be encouraging even when it's difficult and you've had a rough day. I've watched what my wife has been through and how much studying it took for her to learn how to live with this disease. She's seen many specialists only to find out all the things she was going through had to be related to Alpha-gal. Her doctor wanted a second opinion due to her many symptoms. We traveled to Memphis twice to see an anaphylaxis specialist, only to be told to find something enjoyable to do at home and stay away from crowds. He couldn't explain her high numbers with all the precautions she was already taking. We love to travel in our RV and enjoy life while keeping her safe. Live every day to the fullest. Be supportive. Stay safe."

Sources for more information:

https://www.cdc.gov/ticks/alpha-gal/index.html

https://tbcunited.org/

https://www.facebook.com/groups/alphagalsupport/

http://www.thealphagalkitchen.com/home.html

https://www.facebook.com/groups/119373192002966

https://snacksafely.com/2019/07/qa-everything-you-need-to-know-alpha-gal-syndrome-the-meat-allergy-you-can-catch/

https://www.facebook.com/groups/311221623112326

http://www.liebellclinic.com/

www.ingramcontent.com/pod-product-compliance
Lightning Source LLC
Chambersburg PA
CBHW072103150726
47999CB00005B/1863